Corporate Command
+
Control
+
Eject

- Dori Molla -

VSW ArtHouse
Brooklyn, NY

Copyright © 2022
by VSW ArtHouse

VSW ArtHouse
P.O. Box 20143
Brooklyn, NY 11202

All rights reserved. No part of this publication may be reproduced, distributed, or transmitted in any forms or by any means, including photocopying, recording, or other electronic or mechanical methods, without the prior written permission of the publisher, except in the case of brief quotations embodied in critical reviews and certain other noncommercial uses permitted by copyright law.

For permission requests, contact the Publisher.

ISBN: 978-1-7357539-1-1

CONTENTS

I.	8/17
II.	The Ask
III.	Minor Details
IV.	Last September
V.	The Waiting Game
VI.	All Bets In
VII.	Photogenic
VIII.	Final Decision
IX.	Leadership Principles
X.	Covid-19
XI.	Erratic
XII.	Lean In
XIII.	Weakest Link
XIV.	Chief People Officer
XV.	Accidental Death and Dismemberment
XVI.	Bottom Line
XVII.	Personal Note
XVIII.	Copy and Paste
XIX.	WTF
XX.	Awareness Program
XXI.	Women Need Not Apply
XXII.	Conversation
XXIII.	A Few Words
XXIV.	A Short Story About Humans
XXV.	Rat Race
XXVI.	Continued Friendship
XXVII.	Reference
XXVIII.	Special
XXIX.	Mental
XXX.	EDI
XXXI.	Rave Reviews
XXXII.	Next
XXXIII.	2/18
XXXIV.	Into the Woods

XXXV.	AF Environment
XXXVI.	FYI
XXXVII.	Bottomless Ocean
XXXVIII.	Simple Solutions
XXXIX.	Cardi B
XL.	10,000 Pennies
XLI.	Smooth
XLII.	Write Off
XLIII.	Indecent Exposure
XLIV.	Wasted
XLV.	Inspiring Immigrant
XLVI.	At 17
XLVII.	Final Act
XLVIII.	Sealed
XLIX.	Far away
L.	One Small Step
LI.	Forget
LII.	For Review and Approval
LIII.	Pride Fest
LIV.	Coldest
LV.	Never Ever
LVI.	American Triumph
LVII.	Botched
LVIII.	The Only One
LIX.	Ruined
LX.	Capitalism 101
LXI.	F*ck You
LXII.	Tribeca Film Festival
LXIII.	Finding Jesus
LXIV.	Opportunities
LXV.	E-Shame
LXVI.	The Power of Narrative
LXVII.	Prayer
LXVIII.	The Great Resignation
LXIX.	Low Expectations
LXX.	Confidential
LXXI.	Exotic Bird

LXXII.	Pronouns
LXXIII.	Fleeing
LXXIV.	Promotions
LXXV.	Smell Test
LXXVI.	Google Sheets
LXXVII.	IDGAF – The Corporate Edition
LXXVIII.	Realizations
LXXIX.	Brooklyn Accent
LXXX.	Tanglewood
LXXXI.	A Lil' Bit
LXXXII.	212 Area Code
LXXXIII.	Blood and Tears
LXXXIV.	Around Here
LXXXV.	Survey
LXXXVI.	Take Care/Give Care
LXXXVII.	Missing Part
LXXXVIII.	Spiegel im Spiegel
LXXXIX.	Proceed with Caution

8/17

First day. New job. Same old me. 24 years of age. 20 pounds lighter. White cotton shirt. Is it too wrinkled? Am I sweaty? Dewy-eyed walking nervously around Washington Square Park. It is a sticky and stinky New York morning. Just like I like it. Not the stinky part. Only the summertime sunny excerpt. It makes for a good day ahead, at least in my book. "I shouldn't show up at the office an hour early on my first day," I thought to myself. It would make me look desperate. I feel excited more than desperate. And my excitement is mine to savor.

At 14, I did tell my physics teacher that I'd be going to New York. That was only wishful thinking on my part. Now I was about to start my first real job. In New York City. I'd be learning and dedicating my time to greatness. It was the level of greatness that justified a salary way lower than the cost of living in the city or outside of it. Forget about school loans and any spare dreams. But idealists don't give a damn about money. Then again, sacrifice builds character and money doesn't qualify as real sacrifice.

Note to self: Be curious and on the lookout for brilliant works by anyone from every corner of the world. How many names was I going to memorize in the first week? I was about to embark on a journey accompanied by creativity reflecting the countless vibes, events, and quests of modern time. My eyes already caught Alvin Singleton's *Extension of a Dream*. What a dream!

The Ask

You have to believe me. This is not even about money. Although it is about money because nothing is free and the company never offers deep discounts for esteemed works by esteemed creators. I have built a reputation of high standards on behalf of a company that has continuously shortchanged me. I am not even greedy. I really, truly am a generous person in thoughts and actions. I am a simple human living a simple life of mundane day to day occurrences. However, at this point, it is way overdue to ask for what I deserve. I deserve my fair share of recognition and compensation for everything I do.

My list of responsibilities goes above and beyond my actual title and compensation. My professional profile is that of someone who finds solutions. I am someone who is knowledgeable, reliable and someone who cares. I am passionate about helping everyone and making a difference. That has been me for the last 17 years. That's who I am. Nobody can deny it. Dial anyone right this minute. Send a survey to any institution, organization, or agency in the client or partner list anywhere in the country or the world.

I have been running a one woman show for too long. I have shown resilience during times of crisis. I have initiated, negotiated, and finalized a staggering number of contracts. I have reviewed, approved, managed media inquiries, editorial and production questions, logistics and production issues. I have my eyes glued to two monitors and a never ending priority list that nobody can manage better than me.

In addition to everything I have mentioned so far, don't forget that I am the sole client-facing, problem solver for accounting matters. I am the one who ran and presented 100% of financial, performance and promotion reports.

I work with various offices and teams to get bits and pieces of details creating complete pictures and offering concrete solutions. I address inquiries by executive directors, finance and accounting managers, managing directors, industry experts, performers, marketing and media teams in North America and beyond. I have continuously adapted seamlessly to an ever-changing environment where what's in today is out tomorrow.

One of my main responsibilities is to ensure that full credit and fair compensation is given to the appropriate creator. Why should I not ask for full credit and fair compensation for myself based on my very own long list of contributions?

Minor Details

Some details are easy to forget. Some are left out on purpose. May I remind you of a recent event of no small consequence? Do you recall the new hire who felt overwhelmed by the magnitude of the work as an assistant? The company pushed me to bully the new hire. I declined.

A VP of HR emailed me after 5 o'clock on a Friday. It was the VP's day off. She had to show me who was the boss. She said that she didn't understand what I wrote. She wanted me to report to her whether or not I completed the task that she had assigned to me. Is that standard VP of HR conduct shooting emails of that nature after 5 on a Friday? Again, it was her day off. She must have been really irritated or bored to take time from her day off to put me in my place of invisibility once and for all.

A couple of weeks later, another VP of HR was on the other line but she showed no interest in what I had to say. I let her know that it is my firm belief that all people should be treated with respect. Respect is a basic requirement for every level of communication. But the HR position was clear: I should go along with what I am told. In the end, the company's interests come first. If they had to fire the new hire for poor performance, the company would have to pay that person severance pay. It is the corporate way of doing business, I was told. The company avoids being sued by paying out severance pay even for poor performance. It is an added protection mechanism during times of uncertainty. HR knows best.

I declined to act as a bully on behalf of the company. I did not appreciate being bullied either. You preferred that I kept quiet when I was being harassed. I could not. Many phone calls, emails and texts were sent even to my personal phone.

In the end, a couple of months later, the new hire left on good terms, praising me for my mentorship and support. Did the company take note of that?

In conclusion, I make money for the company. I save money. I build relationships.

My ask is simple: full credit for everything I do and fair compensation which is merit based. Ah, I am being a nuisance, you say. How so?

Why am I given the run around here? I never treat anyone with this level of disregard and disrespect. Why am I being pushed around like this? What's up?! The corporate world is tough, you say. What's so hard about giving me what I deserve?

Last September

Didn't we have a conversation in September? Didn't I make it clear that the situation at work had become intolerable for me? Every single day I was the default go-to person for a million tasks from every department.

Urgent! We need these reports asap for a meeting tomorrow morning!
Urgent! This order and this one and that one must be sent out soon!
Urgent! Editorial issues ought to be addressed now!
Urgent! Account reconciliation must be resolved immediately!
Urgent! Transfer of materials must be confirmed asap!

So many urgent inquiries from all sides and only one of me. Nobody worried about the million and one things I had to do for my own department.

I cried in September. I felt defeated. I felt cornered. Nobody cared. Not a single person. Why? I asked for change. Change is a weird thing to ask for when the majority does not benefit from it. But this change was overdue. Change is usually overdue. So, patience is required. I have been patient. Logging in 17 years of patience. Back in September I was told that it was possible to work something out. I was told that the higher ups were aware of what was going on with me. I was told that they were understanding and supportive. Naïve people like me can be lied to their faces and nothing comes of it. How fun!

I heard not a single word after September. No follow up regarding my request. Nothing even before the winter break. Not a single line of email to say, "Happy Holidays! Let's touch base in 2022 to follow up on what was discussed in September." My situation must have served as free entertainment, I guess.

Despite my profound disappointment, I did not let any of our clients or partner agencies get a sense of what was going on. I kept doing my work as usual. Still, being openly ignored was not a nice way to end the year, was it? Nobody appreciates being treated like a fucking joke. Wouldn't you agree?

The Waiting Game

Questioning myself

Was this part of your dream? 17 years and begging to be acknowledged for your contribution based on your dedication, the quality of your performance and expertise accumulated in the course of almost two decades.

Do you regret not turning on your camera during that important teams meeting with the VP & SVP? Wasn't that the most important meeting of the year? Didn't you unplug the wall mounted Dyson in the background? What if they noticed the Dyson squeezed next to the heavy loaded bookcase, you thought? You even wore a dark, high collar shirt for serious vibes.

Camera off. Gloves on. Let's get ready to rumble. And rumble we did.

Knowing that they won't budge...

Well, the SVP did not turn on his camera. It felt weird having my camera on while his was off. I turned mine off, too. The VP was a few minutes late. He had a fake, blurry background. I didn't see a point in turning my camera on again.

And, I do not have a poker face. Can you imagine me reacting to being called "emotional" when I brought up that performance review grading system?

It sounds like a pathetic point but it needed to be addressed. I was graded a 3 during the first performance review. 3 meant excellent. I was a 3. I was graded a 2 on the second performance review. I asked why a lower grade the second time around. I was told that as per HR a 3 is given only to top brass executives who are the movers and shakers of the company. I shared my unanswered question - "Why 2?" - with my uninterested audience of two men.

Does anyone review the VP's and SVP's performances? Are they automatically a 3? "If I am never to earn a 3, but my performance review is to play a role in my career advancement, how am I to move up the ranks? Is there even a path forward or upward or whatever?"

"You are being so emotional about this," shot back the SVP. The VP shook his head in agreement. "C'mon why bring this up? I thought we put this to sleep."

They admitted that the grading system was called controversial by some. It was not meant to be taken seriously.

Maybe that was a stupid move on my part. But what about fairness?
Bitch, please!

My string of stupid moves did not end there.

I also mentioned the job posting that I received in my inbox months earlier. Last summer, the company posted a job ad seeking a Senior VP of streaming with 10-12 years of industry experience. The position would be filled by a good negotiator who had the ability to collaborate easily with internal and external stakeholders. I repeated that I have 17 years of experience negotiating, communicating and connecting the dots and helping people from one continent to another. At that point, my audience of two must've reached the highest level of boredom. Sigh. Hmmm. Silence.

Finally, I asked both gents for advice. What would they do in my place? Silence. Again.

A faint counter offer came through: same title, a tad, not too much but something of a raise. Would I go for that?

"No."

N to the fucking O. I was and I still am 100% certain of that NO.

Here pussy, pussy, pussy. Here's your chow. You want salmon instead of this canned shit in a dingy plastic bowl. Sure, you do. Too bad. Your loss.

My crooked universe...

The normal course of business in many fields, including the art world, is simple and clear: women should shut up. Women should put up with what they are served. Straight shooters like me are despised. I am a headache to the upper echelon. Not very ladylike to talk about titles, money and benefits, is it?

What helps my case? I don't have a fucking case. Nobody gives two shits about my performance or my years of experience. I am so annoying to you when I mention my situation. I have a fucking accent. Why is it so hard to understand, you ask? Who has time to waste talking to me and listening to me complain about how I am underemployed and underpaid?

How about some fucking gratitude on my part? I have been shown plenty of generosity, haven't I? I have been allowed in certain restricted areas. I got plenty of teams and zoom invites to work centric discussion tables in the previous year. I was the only one providing information with concrete details to workflow related questions, wasn't I? So, what? How is that weird? Aren't superiors meant to just be spectators? Don't they do enough just by looking superior?

Apparently, none of what I say matters. It is frowned upon to ask to be credited in full and compensated fairly for your work. Especially if you are a woman.

I am invisible from dawn to dusk if the superior gentle folk say it is so. I see a couple of lackeys of the fair sex by their side. The boss ladies close their eyes, cover their ears, and shut their mouths when someone like me speaks up. The workload was mine and mine alone to carry. I was being an inconvenience to the higher ups: men and 1 or 2 women. They probably wondered why I had to ruin such a good thing for them. Why insist on being credited in full and being paid fairly?

My reputation was that of a hardworking, selfless idiot of no weight.

I was a mother, they said.

Mothers are caring. They should be nurturing and selfless. Mothers have clear priorities: kids and Sunday dinners.

What the hell was I doing asking for a promotion and salary to match my actual contribution? Why was I being so difficult? Why did I have to be such a killjoy?

Another sticky note to my idiot self:

When you see a job posting for a VP or a Senior VP, consider saving your fucking time by not applying for it. Women Need Not Apply. It's an unspoken rule. VPs and especially SVPs do not get jobs through job postings anyway. That's particularly true for women of no provenance, women with no significant connections, no trophy husbands or wives. But I fucking have a trophy husband who is super talented and super awesome.

Still unclear....

Fucking hell! I am just being paranoid. Didn't one of the two men say, "I trust we can make it work." Yes, but he had said those same words before. Routine VP remarks for the masses. VPs are never to live up to their word.

The final note from the SPV was, "Why change now? We inherited this situation. We inherited your position. You have always been doing everything. Why change now?"

Hard work and honesty are for dumb - dumbs. You never get far with stupid moves like that. You are a dumb one, my dear.

Why change now? Who the fuck are you to put in a request for change and expect it to be taken seriously?

All Bets In

She
They bet against their best player. You were their fucking VIP. Their quarterback. They thought you were bluffing when you told them that you did not consent to their "Shut Up & Put Up" strategy. It was a bad bet on their part. Their loss.

Me
I cannot fully express the complexity of my feelings right now. Not that I care about "a good bye & thank you for your service" note. But I am owed so much more than that. They all know it. That is the only reason why they will not even write a letter to acknowledge the long list of responsibilities that I covered for so long. I ran quarterly reports. I ran annual and multi-year reports for budget planning and forecasting. I managed 100% of all media requests. I was the only client facing, solution finder for a multitude of subjects. For every subject, actually. All they did was shove me and my request under the rug.

A handful of internal leadership experts decided that the right thing to do was to show me the door since I was not willing to continue playing their game. They must be really proud of themselves and their leadership skills at work. Colleagues representing many amazing organizations call me a dedicated expert with a perfect reputation. Corporate does not care about my colleagues' opinions. I built my professional profile from scratch, completely on my own. Corporate doesn't care about my professional profile. Corporate handled my situation the legal way. What does that even mean? How is it illegal to write a reference letter including the long list of responsibilities that I managed successfully without any real support? Is it because my actual list of responsibilities exceeded the scope of work covered by my title and pay scale?

I listen to a song playing on the radio and I crack a smile. I shouldn't let anybody break my spirit. I got to keep on moving.

But my heart is hurting. My chest feels heavy. I am in pain. On a scale of 1 to 10, it's a solid 10. Did I deserve this sort of ending? Every employee should be treated with respect and dignity, I insist. How can there be change in this world, if people at the top preach change while trying their best to erase every single voice that speaks up in the name of equality? I have been an idiot for so long. 17 years of stupidity will not look good on my LinkedIn profile.

Photogenic

Me
Do you think people who know me directly and indirectly would be surprised by this situation?

Him
Most likely not. Who the fuck do you think you are? Che Guevara? Did you forget how Che died? Che was assassinated in Bolivia. He went there to improve the lives of poor people. He lost. The poor people, those whose lives Che wanted to improve, did not see him as powerful. They turned against him. He was too weak. He was too righteous. The Bolivians knew that they had to stick with the tough crowd.

Fear and strength are part of a winning recipe.

You have nothing to offer without fear and power. Who are your allies? Do you have any? Face some basic facts about who you are and what you have. And move the fuck on.

Me
No, I am no Che Guevara. Che was not asking for a promotion and matching salary for himself. Do I look like I believe in fantasy lands? I asked for a fair share to match my contribution. Nothing more. Nothing less.

It's a punch in the gut to be laughed at and pushed around from this boys' club to the one next door. Don't I deserve better?

If they told me, no, you do not deserve a promotion and matching salary because:

Reason 1
Reason 2
Reason 3

I would consider their reasons to make an informed decision. I voiced my dissent. Their decision was the following:

No, we will not consider your request because you have always done what you do and there is no point to change now.

In other words, take a fucking seat and shut the fuck up. Don't speak until you are spoken to.

Her
Did anyone speak to you like that?

Me
Yes:
No, we will not consider your request because you have always done what you do and there is no point to change now.

No, not with words but with actions:
Take a fucking seat and shut the fuck up. Don't speak until you are spoken to.

For a company that takes pride in empowering voices, it did not take long to silence my voice. They played around and found pleasure in the rejection process.

Him
Maybe you think you are special. You are not. Your story is that of many women, many mothers everywhere. A whole lot of women find themselves even in harsher conditions than yours. Wake the fuck up! Nobody gives a shit. You sound like an entitled little bitch.

Me
I swear, I am not an entitled little bitch. First of all, I ain't little. I might sound like a bitch to you now but I am among the most caring human beings in the world. As for entitled?! C'mon. That's the whole point. If I were entitled, I would not have to jump through these rings of fire. I stayed too long with the same company not because I felt entitled but because staying put gave me the false idea of being in a cocoon. I thought I was protected from the outside world. I have been suffocating in stagnation. At

will. I have worked like a fucking idiot day in and a day out. Even though I never believed the bullshit verbal rewards, I accepted each one with gratitude. "Thank you for your contribution. Your contribution to the greater good is appreciated." "Thank you. Thank you. How fortunate I am to always have so much to do!"

In reality, my workload was insanely dense. I felt its crushing weight and the ticking of time flying by. I felt left behind, stuck in quicksand.

"You're doing great. Keep it up. We're so proud of you." A few important men and a couple of women who stand by their side throw lines like these from time to time. *Meatless bones. Empty shit.*

I am tired of the charade. I am exhausted by the long list of my responsibilities and the lack of acknowledgement. I know the market value of my actual work. I cannot continue keeping my eyes shut to please the corporate demigods. I will not accept my professional fate as written by the almighty corporate czars.

It's weird to look back now that everything is said and done. It feels like I was part of a skivvy operation in a dark alley. I was a speck of dust in the midst of a bunch of righteous liberals and proud progressives raising their voices for a just world.

I'll reach out to a few people. Just to hear their perspective. Isn't 2022 the year of focusing on Equality. Diversity. Inclusion. Show me the facts. Don't just share your cheap propaganda pamphlets.

Her
You're so delusional, darling. EDI is not about you. How can you even think that anyone will care?

Me
There's that young woman. 10 years ago, I thought we could be friends. Our names were connected because of work. We are not friends. She might not even recognize me if I reached out to her directly. However, in recent years her name has come up quite a lot. Her work has gotten attention from various groups. A few

influential men dismissed her talent saying, "She is photogenic. She looks good in pictures. It's good for us that she is making the news." That's the portrait of a woman in the 21st century. Photogenic qualities are acknowledged. Talent and abilities are quickly dismissed. Me on the other hand, I ain't even photogenic. Big nose. Big glasses. Frizzy hair. I've made plenty of money for the company, haven't I?

What if I reached out to her? What if I share this story with her?

Him
What fucking support? What the fuck are you talking about? Do you fucking know who the fuck you are? You are Ms. Little Nobody. Even if your imaginary friend there said yes, what would the two of you do? Go out in the street, join forces with other inspired females, mothers, dog mothers, cat mothers, motherless mothers, emancipated women, transgender women, young debutantes, immigrant women and their inspired saviors? Will the whole bunch of you change the world in unity?

Wake the fuck up! You and your photogenic friend ain't worth shit.

Final Decision

11:30 am. Phone call. No teams. Easier. Chattier. Friendlier.
I did not take a shower. Just me with my knotted hair in my oversized t-shirt and 5-year-old culottes. I didn't wake up feeling particularly optimistic. Neither particularly VP material.

The previous Thursday I emailed the grainy background gent reminding him about my ask. "My situation is not being taken seriously. My status quo is working fine for everyone but me." He wrote back assuring me that I had nothing to worry about. The SVP, who was the main negotiator, and the COP (Chief of People) were talking and I'd hear back soon. Of course, he said. I was being taken seriously. *As always*.

On Friday, the main negotiator emailed me after 5 o'clock and we agreed on a phone call, Monday at 11:30.

How about a suspenseful weekend? That's an added bonus you know. Corporate does that for you. You don't have to pay a subscription fee for stuff like that. And it's as real as it gets. Corporate delivers high intensity suspense - free of charge.

The conversation started on a friendly note. How are the kids? How's the family? I knew in my bones that none of this small talk was coming from a place of honesty. Usually sweet words, out of the blue like that, are not a good sign. The thought process of the bullshitter probably goes along these lines: Let me be nice for a sec. It'll help neutralize the pain soon after I stab the unsuspecting subject with my mighty dagger.

My suspicion turned out to be true. Right on the money. The short story was short, but not sweet. No, the COP saw no reason for change. There was no budget for change. I should continue working as I had done so far. Frankly, my 17 years were my relationship with two men: the grainy background guy and the one who operates mostly behind the scenes. Corporate got nothing to offer. Corporate got nothing to do with me. I was inherited. My position was part of a deal. It was a deliberate and conscious choice. A corporate choice.

The long story was long and it pointed to a long road to nowhere. Stick around longer and something may come up. No meaningful change in six months or a year but something further down the line. The conversation could stay open. Corporate knows.

I said that I'm not a quitter. Not a quitter in name or nature. This is me being thrown out, just like that, I said.

I spoke my words as clearly as possible and without a doubt in my mind. Not only did I not cry, but there was no quivering or trembling. My heart was about to jump out of my chest though. But my heart is not a corporate concern.

Maybe staying around until March makes sense. It's when they give out bonuses. Maybe they'll give you something.

HA!

There is no sticking around if everything is to remain the same for me while it continues to be an easy ride as usual for the rest of you. Get paid the big money, show off your big titles and bask in the glory of your success.

Imagine! A woman has had enough of her abusive relationship of 17 years. She says as much. Her abusive partner says, 'why change now, babe? We've done the same shit for so long. It's the only fucking way you know. Why not keep it going for as long as it's convenient for me? What is it to you? You know how to do it all with your eyes closed? It's me or the highway, babe. The highway is cold and crazy."

Sometimes the highway is the only choice, babe, I say.

Leadership Principles

1. Flex your power muscle. Intimidate those who play crucial roles in your universe.

2. Make quick decisions without thinking about immediate or long term impact.

3. Do not listen but always dictate and give orders.

4. Forget data and facts. Make biased decisions to silence calls for equal and fair treatment.

5. Never venture out of your comfort zone.

6. Ignore talent and dedication. Surround yourself with people who only say "yes sir" and "yes ma'am".

7. Avoid responsibility. Deny dialogue. Seize control.

8. Prevent change at all costs.

9. Disregard measurable effects of your decision-making powers.

10. Impress yourself and your buddies with quick witted lingo that shuts down any internal player of no consequence.

Covid-19

The first two weeks of the new year I was out due to Covid-19. It was overwhelming to log in at work after 12 days of isolation. What mayhem! More than a thousand emails. Hundreds of overdue inquiries. Tens of voicemails. What happened? Why were clients and their requests ignored for the entire time that I was out? It was a serious health situation. Covid-19! Even if I had been out of the office on vacation, inquiries should not have been put on hold until I returned. It's not like the money from these inquiries was going into my bank account. All that business meant more dollars for the corporate coffers, didn't it? How disheartening! What if I had died? If I had died, the company would've probably ordered a funeral wreath and shared their thoughts and prayers. Death seems like the easy way out sometimes, doesn't it?

I received a personal email from a team member offering to entertain my kids on zoom so I could catch up with work. It was a well-meaning offer from a friend, wasn't it? Yeah, but my work hours are 9-5. My kids and my family are not interfering with my work life whatsoever. My work life is absolutely interfering with my home life.

I have nothing left to prove at work. There is no recognition. There is no incentive. There is no intention to help me have a visible presence. There is no plan to pay me fairly for the million and one things I do. Why bother continuing to strive hard to be the last in the totem pole?

The SVP said that he gets it. He mentioned that if he were a friend he'd say that this job was making me miserable. I decided not to share that this situation was making me physically sick. He mentioned that he'd think of other companies in the industry for me to consider. At the same time, his advice was that I stick around until March or so. *That's when the company gives out bonuses. Maybe they'll give you something.*

"Maybe is no good, baby," I said to myself. March feels so far away. No fucking way. People please, stop pulling my chain!

Cut the fucking chains and run free, bitch. Running wild is better than a slow death in the heart of darkness in an endless uber liberal wasteland.

Disengagement between various vital parts of a living organism will result in failure.

I am sinking in here. No light at the end of the tunnel. No empathy. No comradery. What's the point? How many lives do I have left to live? How many years? Is it worth being miserable day in and day out?

Erratic

It ain't erratic behavior if a worthless earthling like me says to the big bosses, "That's it. Give me what I deserve or we go our separate ways. Reason for separation: irreconcilable differences after 17 years in an unconventional union."

I wish I had Snoop's dance moves. Despite my modest dance skills, I know a good beat when I hear one. There are so many good tunes to cheer me up.

Jay-Z's *Dirt Off Your Shoulder* is my anthem right about now.

Put it on and turn it up! *Dirt Off Your Shoulder* and a river of tears for breakfast and lunch. Dinnertime is reserved for my kids. My babies have nothing to do with my misery. They deserve better.

Lean In

Request to lean in: Dismissed. Denied.

Who leans in on whom?
What do women do when they fail to find anywhere to lean in?
Where do you lean in? Where do I lean in? Where does she lean in? Where do they lean in? Where do we lean in?
Why is leaning in not an option available to all women?
How to increase lean in opportunities for every woman?

Women deserve full credit and equal pay. Where do they lean in to achieve such things in 2022?

Weakest Link

The Corporate Demigods
We celebrate artistry. This woman is raising a stink about a whole lot of nothing. She is getting paid to learn and to represent works by geniuses. She plays a teeny tiny, miniscule supporting role. It's the superbly talented humans we care about. We have no time to waste with weak links. Actually, change that to *the weakest link among us*.

She
I ain't the weakest link. I'm telling you. Believe me. Can't they see their level of dishonesty? The double standards. How could they be messing with people like this?

My solid work record and a long list of connections around the world cannot be erased by HR gurus, VPs or SVPs.

Facts over false narratives!

Chief People Officer

A: Does your company have a Chief People Officer?

B: No. Does yours?

A: Yes.

B: What does a Chief People Officer do?

A: I don't know. I haven't seen one in action.

B: But you said you know one.

A: I know of one but I don't know one. The one and only who I have come across avoided people. Or avoided me. Maybe she did not see me as "people".

B: That's great!
Chief People Officer – Job Requirement – Avoid People
Concentrate on being a chief. What's the purpose of a chief?

A: I'll get back to you if I ever find out. From now on, I'm gonna avoid anyone who dangles a Chief People Officer title at me. Although, there might be decent Chiefs of People out there. I reserve the right to change my opinion if I am given reason to do so down the road.

Accidental Death and Dismemberment

I tried to take the whole conversation seriously but it was impossible. A VP of HR called on teams. Camera off. It's probably an HR department policy. No face time even on teams. I guess it was better that way. I would've burst out laughing. Looking at her profile picture, she seemed okay. A bit stressed out. Her voice was shaky. Maybe a bad connection. What a metaphor!

No conversation. Straight to the point.

HR: No severance pay because the company did not terminate you. You quit. You resigned.

Me: I did not quit. I did not resign. The load of work is unacceptable for my current title and compensation. The company did not want to make any changes to match my long list of responsibilities, performance level, and years of experience. The company basically threw me out. There's a difference between that and quitting.

HR: No. You resigned because we did not fire or terminate you. Your last date is 2/18.

Me: K.

HR: Accidental death and dismemberment. Let's talk about accidental death and dismemberment. So, your insurance coverage for accidental death and dismemberment started on...Let me see. I might be looking at the wrong forms here. Accidental death and dismemberment insurance coverage ends the week of 2/18. It could be 2/28. Did you have accidental death and dismemberment insurance? Maybe it is not applicable. I will check our records again. As of now, the question about your accidental death and dismemberment remains open.

Bottom Line

All Flags Waving High

We care. We are open minded. We are conscious. We acknowledge the impact of our actions. We promote diversity. We celebrate women. Black History Month programming is our top priority. Indigenous Day. Latin culture is our focus. Asian Heritage month. LGBTQ+ we see you. Love is Love. Immigrants. You inspire us. We salute you all. Visibility. Voices. Inclusivity.

When the Curtains Fall

The bottom line is that profit is all that matters. Making money is good. Spending money is bad. Ignore little minions asking to be credited in full and compensated fairly for their work. Their voices must be silenced.

What makes economic sense? What do algorithms say? Who gets celebrated? Who gets shut out?

Corporate wants to ensure you that you are of no consequence. Only high-level players matter. Do you matter to corporate? Money makers matter. Only money matters. Who serves the bottom line? Big names. Big money. Money makes money. Money loves money. More money. More. More. More money.

Personal Note

From: A Special Friend

Listen, you know how much I care about you. I know you and your family. Keep that in mind. Are you sure that your decision is the right one for you and your family?

No reference letter will be issued on behalf of the company. It is a legal matter. Nobody is above the law. On a personal note, we can discuss details later.

I care about you very much.

Copy and Paste

Me
How dare you write anything and sign my name? How dare you ask that I copy and paste your words and send them as mine?

Him
It's not a big deal. It's common practice. It's a mechanism to protect corporate. This is corporate. You should get used to it. It's not worth asking too many questions.

She
Voicemails. Texts. Emails
Call me now. Here is my cell phone again. I am waiting for your call. Call me.

Me
I do not get intimidated easily. She does not have a problem with me, you say. But her conduct is not professional. Her approach is out of line. Her communication style is unacceptable. You do not write your words and add my name demanding that I go along with your intimidation tactics.

WTF

Them
We keep things confidential. We hurt and squeeze and suffocate. We do it all under saturated backgrounds and big smiles and touched up photos of happy people.

Who the fuck do you think you'll impress with your bullshit requests for visibility and equality? If you get out of here, you'll die.

Don't look up! The light is blinding. Don't look outside of this imaginary circle of fake brotherhood and sisterhood! If you do, you'll disappear. I'm telling you. You're making a big mistake. A huge mistake. Only dumb people leave a comfortable spot like this. A comfort zone is hard to find. Once you find it, you can sink in it forever. Who the fuck do you think you are?

Me
Who the fuck do you think you are? You flex your muscles and remind me that death is imminent if I leave this pretentious phony paradise. It's not impressive behavior. We are all mortals here. Look at the state of affairs in this country and around the world! Do you see any connection between failed power plays and turmoil? WTF!

Awareness Program

Him
You know the friends who care about you but do not really give a shit? You know the people who throw you off a speeding train and then cry at your funeral? Members of that crowd make speeches about keeping you in their thoughts and prayers. They will say they miss you as they take a big dump on your grave.

They are fake friends - by choice. Don't blame them. Don't waste your time with them.

Her
Believe me. I am so very sorry to see you leave. I hope we can remain friends as we have over the course of many years.

Him
They'll say it was emotional exhaustion that caused her to turn her back on her team. She did not turn her back on anybody. She stood up for herself. And what kind of team was hers? A team collaborates and shares responsibilities, doesn't it? We are all being treated *the same* here, they said. *The same* with a few exceptions such as division of work, titles and salaries. What kind of sameness is that?

Her
She felt like an island. She ran a one woman show serving as the main generator of revenue. She made connections worldwide. The others held their titles tight. They saved their fine salaries. They complained of the unbearable weight of self-importance. They let corporate worry about the rest.

Different platforms. Different objectives. Different perspectives. Alternate realities.

Women Need Not Apply

Backroom deals do not require the presence of women. If women are part of any high-stake discussion, they better sign an NDA. Swiftly. They get limited clearance. Always. They are not to show interests beyond their gender limitations. They are not to ask questions about important affairs.

Women are welcome to cry hard when other women lose political or other races. Women are encouraged to act outraged when they hear outrageous things.

Doing outrageous things, such as asking to be credited in full for their work, is not ladylike. This type of behavior is frowned upon.

Women should never pursue equal pay for equal work.

If you come across women who express unhealthy ambitions, make it clear to them that they do not belong among us: the glorious saviors of humanity who set standards of leadership without emotional attachments to things, events and/or people.

Positions of power are not intended for women. They are high stress and high pressure. We are looking out for women's health and sanity by holding them back. Yes, their workloads may be heavy at times but they are deemed appropriate for good reason.

Women need not apply for leadership positions. Leadership skills transform the second sex. Not for the better.

The desire to lead will mess up women's brains. It will make them go wild. Unhealthy yearnings for power are detrimental to women's health.

The future may be female. But men dictate the past, present and future.

Conversation

Him
That sounds pretty shitty.

Her
It was. It is.

Him
What do you plan to do?

Her
Test that recipe that's promoted as Norman Rockwell's favorite oatmeal and raisin cookie recipe.

Him
Good. Forget about these MFs. They ain't worth it.

Her
True. I feel cheated. We didn't have to agree. After 17 years, we should've been able to work out something before going our separate ways with a "thanks & good luck".

Him
Conscious uncoupling on an institutional level.

Her
Indeed. Why not? Everyone wins. I mean 17 years of history cannot be erased just like that.

Him
You might start considering that.

Her
Erasing my past? I did not do anything wrong. What is my crime?

Him
There is no need for crime for there to be punishment and suffering of any kind. That's not new.

A Few Words

Part of me is crushed. Part of me is elated. Part of me is sad. Part of me is hopeful.

Take stock of your actions. Make your presence felt. Confirm that your voice cannot be dismissed easily. Do not go quietly into the night.

The ending was a ridiculously dramatic production. A complete failure, by any accounts, sponsored by a self-proclaimed generous bunch. Did they ever say that they believe in a world that gives credit where credit is due?

A Short Story About Humans

They are born alone and defenseless. They cry. They surrender. They betray. They hate. They fuck up. They fear. They love. Sometimes. They have separation issues.

Rat Race

If you got no "*fuck you money*" you are part of a rat race. Where do bitches fit in a rat race? I am not qualified to speak on that subject.

I remember taking a part-time job at a well-known quick fashion store in 2007. Was I a full-time worker in the publishing world then? Yes. The salary from my full-time work was not sufficient to rent an apartment under my name. I could not afford rent with my salary. I wanted to make some extra money so I got a part time job. Woo-hoo me! 70+ hour work week to make me feel extra wanted everywhere.

Britney's *Work Bitch* is blasting on my speakers right now.
I didn't want no Maserati or Bugatti or Lamborghini in 2007. I don't want them now. Neither can I afford one.

I want a martini. Dirty. I'll keep working. In my dreams, I'll wear black or a wine color gown. In reality, I'll be in my jeans and cotton shirt of choice in front of my mac.

I was advised not to work like a bitch though. It's better to work like a bastard. Working like a bitch ain't got nobody far.

I digress...New York City rats are fat. The rat race here is vicious. Some would say more so than anywhere else. Why bother with the rat race? Isn't it wiser to be a fat cat lounging around, savoring solitude?

Remember that fat cat that always made an unsolicited appearance at a monthly Zoom meeting? People have made many questionable choices of zoom backgrounds. Was there an underlying meaning of that zoom view of a bedroom with a full view of a disinterested fat cat on top of a few shiny pillows?

That fat cat was not disinterested. She was cracking up. That fat cat was fucking laughing at the imbeciles on the screen struggling to prove their worth in a rat race of losers. I was one of the imbeciles completely in awe of the fat cat.

Continued Friendship

Reach out to me with a reference letter request after your last day of service with the company. I am looking forward to the next phase of our continued friendship.

Ha! The reply that will be stuck in the draft folder forever included a couple of pathetic lines such as the following:

...continued friendship – is it based on concealing some naked truths of a certain value...

Reference

Asking for a reference letter from the people on the podium was more like begging for a consolation prize for my bruised soul. It was also an opportunity for the esteemed leaders to do the right thing. "No can do," was their unanimous reply. Company policy and legal procedures were given as reasons for the denied request.

If there is nothing to hide, nothing to conceal, why not issue a letter confirming who I was, what I did and how I performed for 17 years?

I should have settled for nothing less than Chief Problem Solver. I am not talking about potential. My request was based on my actual performance and productivity level. Deny it if you can. I was the sole client facing representative working with all internal teams and partner agencies in daily communication with thousands of contacts in North America and around the world. But don't you worry about that reference letter. Clients and business partners from this country and other countries in different continents have reached out to me already. They all know it that you trying to cover up your nickel and diming ways is at the heart of your reference letter denial. It ain't right. Who cares about what's right, you say?

Special

Them
You ain't special. We are special. It's a hard life and you ain't seen a thing. You have it easy. It's tough out there.

Me
This is not about me being special. This is about me getting full credit and fair compensation for everything that I have done and continue to do.

They say that they are special because they believe that they hold my fate in their hands. But they do not.

It took only 17 years to clarify that.

Us
Wouldn't you feel devalued if you weren't credited in full for your work? Why is it wrong to ask for fair and equal compensation?

Them
That's how it is for the majority of people. It is especially true for women. It's sad that you just learned that now, in your fourth decade on this planet. Shame! Shame!

Mental

Women go mental just like that. Look at her. Why did she have to share some stupid details about her stupid work life? It involves a single person and a single company, doesn't it? WGAFF: Who Gives a Flying Fuck! Does she think she'll change the course of history? The idiot!

I might not change the course of history. I am not going to keep quiet. I won't play by the rules of a game that is rigged. Many nights my kids have had only a bowl of cereal instead of a proper dinner so I could work and work and work. Sometimes until 9 pm. 9 am until 9 pm was never my schedule. I guess I worked those crazy hours at will. How inconvenient of me to mention stupid stuff like that?

EDI

She
What is EDI?

He
Electronic Data Interchange

She
Well, I was thinking more along the lines of Equality. Diversity. Inclusion.

He
Why does it matter?

She
Who knows? Another mechanism to help the world become a fairer place. Maybe it is doomed to fail.

What would be a good twitter intro for EDI? EDI – no clue but look it up. If it makes sense to you, adopt an EDI mentality.

Rave Reviews

I.

We walk side by side for a stretch of time. Quite a long stretch. There are storms and dry spells. Somehow, we make it from one adventure to the next. Suddenly, we find ourselves in the midst of a strange and unknown territory. You have to lose the extra weight to sail further. Off the boat you throw me. Soon after your strategic move, I am told to save the fucking boat. "Fuck rave reviews. No fucking reviews will be issued," you yell as you see me disappear.

II.

Her
Can they buy rave reviews about their illustrious history?
It is a possibility, isn't it?

Him
Your work affected others directly. People around the globe know you. You will get rave reviews from verified users.

To follow a sense of decorum, many ex-employees decline to comment about their treatment at their jobs. But the great resignation is not a coincidence. That is a statement in and of itself.

You will be ok. Many people will gladly stand up for anyone with a solid track record. You have a solid track record.

Next

What comes next?
IDK

How will your game strategy change on your next adventure?
I got no game.

Next time someone tells you to trust them, will you?
Hmmm. Like in *Gomorrah*. When someone said, "Fidati di me", you knew that a bloody scene followed. Believe me! I'll betray you the first chance I get, they said. They did. They tried to blame others. Who cares! I won't trust anyone to the extent that I trusted them. That's a promise to myself - for the rest of my life. I keep my promises.

In your next lifetime, you'll be better prepared to face the world.
Don't care!

Seating next to each other for so long and being complete strangers the entire time. How about that?
AKA: Wake-up call!

2/18

It marks the end of an era.

4,100 days.
98,400 hours.
590,4000 minutes.
354,240,000 seconds.

No blood was spilled. A bleeding heart does not count. Tears were shed. Curse words were thrown in private. Laughter was heard. Stories developed. Experiences piled up. In the end, heavy doors were shut abruptly.

A shadow existence melting away on a cold February day.

Into the Woods

Into the woods. Getting lost in nature. The snow looks beautiful. Tree branches are heavy and bent by the weight of delicate layers of hardened snow.

I will be fine wiping off boogers, cleaning ears, washing my kids' butts and playing with them as I struggle to hide my trembling hands. I am a natural at making my little ones laugh. Getting better at making yummy lunches will be my top priority in the coming days. My two little tough food critics believe in free speech and they openly express their opinions about food and everything else. Still, they shower me with kisses even when my culinary experiments are not a success. My babies tell me that I am a superwoman. I am no superwoman. I am just a mom. Being a mom is the best title I'll ever hold. Nothing will ever top that. My babies know. Heavy tears slide down my face as I think and cry and walk on the crunchy snow.

I have to clear my head. My heartache will take time to heal. I am hurt. It's not that I failed. It is the level of disdain that I witnessed. Had it been there all along? How did I realize it only now? I have to conceal all this emotional mess. It must be hidden deep down in my chest and in my mind without letting it affect my daily routine.

And rivers run wild as snow melts while the sun pierces through fluffy white clouds. Birds keep singing. Kids keep sharing funny jokes about farts and smelly business. They laugh out loud. Their laughter is music to my ears. Redirecting my attention to what matters most won't be hard with my knuckleheads by my side.

AF Environment

He
To summarize: An asshole free environment is not guaranteed by the law. Obey! Lower your head! Act in humility!

She
I don't believe in fear-based tactics. Their final act of desperation was loosely held together by smoke and mirrors. The final verdict being delivered by someone who could care less about my level of contribution was a bad joke in bad taste, wasn't it?

He
I'll make you a shirt: *Human! Handle with Care. Fragile Contents Inside.*

FYI

People who have impressed me: dedicated professionals who have always managed their responsibilities successfully and worked with integrity. I am impressed by people who treat everyone with respect and dignity. The strivers. The doers. The curious bunch who never give up. They get a standing ovation from me. Small towns. Big cities. I have made real friends everywhere. So many people I care about, collaborated with and helped tirelessly. So many special places. So many special moments.

NYC. Boston. LA. D.C. San Fran. Houston. Cincy. Salt Lake City. Cleveland. Philly. Atlanta. Dallas. Seattle. Milwaukee. Chicago. San Diego. Iowa City. San Juan. Boise. Reno. Toronto. Mexico City. Small town USA I love. How many countries? How many continents?

I have connected with scores of incredibly talented and hardworking people who are dedicated to making and sharing beauty and meaning. Real people. Real communities.

Yes, you have made a point casually dropping a famous name here and there. But self-serving celebrity status goes so far. I am in awe of extremely devoted, high achievers working behind the scenes as much as anyone who shines under the spotlight.

Conversations of substance. Gorgeous work by genuine folks. Plenty of treats. I have participated and contributed to it all. Can't take any of it away from me.

Bottomless Ocean

Live Long and Prosper.
One of my colleagues had added that line to her email signature. I had noticed it before but I had not thought much about it. This time it caught my attention. Living long might not be written in the stars for me and that's fine. I just cannot stand the kind of heartache that I am experiencing right now. Prospering is another thing. But you can prosper and forget to live or you can live without prospering. What does it even mean to prosper?

Live as much as you are supposed to live and do the best you can without killing yourself and without hurting others. Selling your soul to the devil in order to secure prosperity is probably not a well thought out plan. How many souls does the devil need, anyway?

This is part of my midday meanderings as I see myself sliding into a bottomless ocean of sadness.

Simple Solutions

Simple solutions are not difficult to find. Some helpful guidelines to consider:

Listen to what is being asked of you
Consider a few available options
Pinpoint one or two doable choices
Don't show up unprepared
Offer a meeting point if you cannot meet the original request
Show empathy and understanding
Be genuinely interested in finding a solution

Cardi B

I have not slept well lately. I have not slept much. I have had all kinds of nightmares. It is not the utter failure of making a good point to get full credit for my work. It is the aftermath. The indecency of it all.

They will provide no comments about my performance of 17 years.

Then Cardi B came to my rescue. At night. In a dream. Imagine Cardi B wasting her time with me. But she did. In my dream. She was the nicest. She listened to me whine. She smiled at me and took my hand. She told me she'd take care of me. Cardi B would be asking a few people at the top to reconsider their position. They'd better give me the glowing reviews that I have earned.

Can you imagine anyone turning down a solid Cardi B request? Nobody would dare.

Cardi B to the rescue. Please, Cardi B. Help me! Thank you!

10,000 Pennies

Mommy, don't worry, I will work and get you 10, no, 100, actually 10,000 pennies. I will give you 10,000 pennies. You don't have to worry, mommy.

Oh, baby! What kind of work will you do to earn 10,000 pennies for mommy?

I'll be an astronaut. I'll be the first human from Brooklyn to step on the moon. Don't worry, mommy!

Smooth

Ma, listen to me. Listen to your oldest son. You have to be smooth. That's it. You're good. I know you. You have me. You have us. We got you, ma. Be smooth!

Write Off

One man cannot write me off.
Two men cannot write me off.
Two men and two women cannot write me off.
Three men and three women cannot write me off.

I cannot be written off that easily.

A whole lot of people, many who have worked with me and many who do not know me at all, might lend me an ear and lend me a hand. They might agree that people who work tirelessly and with dedication deserve full credit and fair compensation for their work. Writing someone off to make a power statement or to focus on profit cannot be that profitable.

People, please do not take pride in writing anyone off!

Indecent Exposure

They must be furious. There was no collegial goodbye. Was she not deserving of one? Why not? Isn't that a final act of desperation on their part? Or a gutsy dare? Dare to leave and you'll see. She might decide to share her side of the story. It may seem like an indecent exposure to some.

Why should they worry if they did nothing indecent? It would be exposure without the indecent part.

Wasted

Critical thinking
Problem solving
Decision making
Leadership skills
Organizational capabilities
Communication abilities
Thriving in a fast-paced, often ambiguous environment
Internal promoter of positive, proactive and productive culture

The above reflect only some core competencies for your job. At the end of your 17-year tenure you will feel like every ounce of your energy was wasted.

Wasted time. Wasted effort. Wasted trust.

Wasted – in a sentence: They wasted their best chance to right their wrong.

Inspiring Immigrant

Covid-19 caused a lot of pain. Lives lost. Dreams interrupted abruptly. Although from a different angle, the global pandemic also triggered an awakening. Injustice could not be hidden or overlooked during lockdown. Protests. Unrest. Solidarity. All in the name of change. Change is good. Except that real change requires real courage and real action, not just slogans.

As it usually happens in times of crisis, numerous opportunists tried to play it smart. Many, who consciously and continuously avoided to lift a finger to help anyone in their own communities, suddenly decided to join popular calls for justice. They added their names to email chains supporting good causes. Deserving causes remain deserving of attention. But yesterday's complicit parties better do some soul searching and some real work before promoting themselves as leaders of change. Haunted by numerous emails with inspiring immigrant stories I jotted down a number of questions that are open for discussion:

Have you read any of the stories in the long email chain with "Inspiring Immigrant Stories" on the subject line?

Have you ever come across an immigrant who made you think like he/she may have an inspiring story to share?

Do you believe inspiring immigrants are real?

Where do you go to interact with an inspiring immigrant?

Why do you avoid paying attention to an inspiring immigrant?

Do you feel irritated or intimidated by inspiring immigrants?

Is it fair to say that the latest global pandemic made it possible for inspiring immigrants to surface?

How do you shut up or shut down an inspiring immigrant?

What is the most egregious request that an inspiring immigrant can make?

Does an inspiring immigrant deserve the spotlight?

At 17

Do you remember yourself at 17?

Red cheeks. Loose curls. Wide eyed. Sitting on a bench at Bryant Park. New York City! How magical! The bus ride from Worcester was brutal. But look at this. You are in New York. The New York City Library is right there. You could spend your entire life in it and be happy. You indulge. People watching. Most rush by. Everyone is busy. Important looking people around here. Will you give it your best shot to make something of yourself in the Big Apple? New York is rough, they say. It seems pretty nice to you. Your gut feeling tells you that NYC is ok with you, too. NYC knows that you, as a newcomer, don't have much to offer for the time being. But maybe NYC will take a chance on you. You have heard that NYC supports dreamers. At 17, all you have is your genuine amazement at this big giant of a city and your light in your naïve eyes dreaming a little dream on a bench at Bryant Park.

Final Act

Silence. No cicadas chirping. Just silence.

She was bound to crash under a curtain of shame. It was a sham! Wouldn't you feel disappointed? People who you considered friends for 17 years were silent as you asked to be credited and paid fairly for your contribution. Silence is a loud statement at times. It was almost debilitating to be part of this final shameless act. It was their final act.

Change of scenery.
Driving away in the snow.
Nature offers the best remedies for a broken heart.

Ping.

A text message.

Don't let this funk get to you, friend. We're here for you.

It was not quite a smile. She was reminded that this was not quite her last act. Not just yet.

Sealed

The records are sealed.

Why do you need to seal records? What's the purpose of sealing records?

Whatever now. Enough with your questions. You will die in infamy.

I will die. You will die. We will all die. The truth will not die with us even if you seal the records.

Far Away

Seating here. Far away from the crash site.

It was a botched assassination attempt. Character assassination. A bunch of dilettantes! Who ideated this poorly planned production?

Eyes glued to the window. A few snowflakes turned into a complete whiteout.

What did the auto-reply say? It was something along the lines of local conditions being the main reason behind the unusual delays.

Welcome this delayed but timely change of scenery!

You have enough energy to survive their spoiled spell. You are far away from it now. Leave it all behind.

Dirt off your shoulder, girl.

One Small Step

One small step for you. Maybe it is a significant step for womenfolk in your area.

Maybe not. It is probably a complete non-event as you say.

Still, it's one small step that gives you freedom.
You have to mourn a bit. 17 years. Take your time. Don't rush.

That one small step will turn out to be one important step. You called them out on their tenacious transgressions. You showed us that you have the brass balls to go all the way. Yours may be categorized as a small step but it is a small step in the right direction. Claim your worth!

Forget

Don't forget what we did for you? We gave you a title. We gave you significance. We paid you what we thought was your value. Fairness and equality are not guaranteed. Don't forget that we know everyone in town. Don't forget that we know the law. Don't forget that without us, you'll drown. You'll die.

We will forget that you ever existed. We will forget that you were here. Will you forget about us?

For Review and Approval

Corporate F*ck Up
Corporate Reject
Corporate Confidentiality
Choose Life Over Corporate
Human! Handle with Care!
Letting Go of Corporate Bliss
Music Executives Kill Music
Elegy for a Tone-Deaf Music World
Corporate Culture vs. Corporate Reality
IDGAF – the Corporate Edition
Woman as Corporate Inheritance
Corporate Culture of Invisibility

Pride Fest

Men and their pride. Ridiculous. At times.

They put on a townhall *teams* meeting that lasts two hours. Brutal. It feels like a bad take on Squid Game. Squid Game: The Corporate World Edition. Who makes it to the end of the game, makes it to the next round. Making it to the next round is the prize. Until you're out. Gather all the helpless nobodies and test them. Speak in monotone voices. Smile with pride. Show off coffered ceilings, crown moldings, gothic windows, elegant backgrounds. Talk about profit. Talk about teams. Talk about your fortunate self.

Instill pride in your pride. Do it! If you see anyone's head start to dangle, know that it is a sign. It is a sign of weakness. Eradicate weakness. Lead with pride!

Coldest

She felt cold. She was freezing. She asked for help. She was dying. She could not die, she told herself. Not without holding her baby in her arms first.

She did not have insurance. No health insurance for ten years. What leverage? She was an *at will* employee. The terms and conditions of her employment were non-negotiable.

When she saw the hospitable bill, she felt the coldest she had ever felt. First bill was more than $60K. Second bill was more than $100K. The company did not support women during their child bearing years.

Some choices are hard. Some decisions require courage. Some interactions showcase the cold-blooded soul crushers among us.

When did you feel the coldest you have ever felt? Has that experience altered you?

Never Ever

Leaky faucets. Peeling ceilings. Big, dusty window with a city view.

A moment of wondering after all the wandering. Do you feel stuck here forever? Didn't you promise yourself that you wouldn't get tangled up? It's written in the cards, they said. You are supposed to take care of everyone but yourself. They are trying hard to convince you that you are being selfish if you ask for full credit for your work as well as fair and equal pay. You are utterly disappointing to them. Make smart choices. Smarter choices.

A reject.
An outcast.
Banned.

Oh my!
Not pretty.
Quite ugly.
The ugliest.

At the eleventh hour, you were asked to share a handbook. A messenger would be urgently sent to your home. 17 years of stellar performance were not part of a handbook. Nobody knew that?

At about two o'clock you are denied access to the email address that you used for 17 years. It was your last Friday using that email. An unforeseen end to a long journey. L'chaim!

You could've never imagined that you'd ever be part of such a messy production. Never ever.

American Triumph

From an angle this is an American tragedy. The one who dedicates her life and energy to the advancement of common good within a confined setting of well-defined borders, gets thrown off the boat without the slightest regard.

Three parties are involved in the fiasco. Seeing the reaction and worrying about the aftermath, the three parties try to blame each other. Whose fault was it? Why was she treated so unfairly? Their main task is to clean up their traces of any wrongdoing. They have to think of a cover up story. They have to concentrate on damage control.

But she is not dead yet. She is not part of only one storyline. The world offers many storylines. She will find herself.

Is it possible that if she speaks up, she might diminish her chances of getting admitted elsewhere? Probably. Or probably not.

The world is made up of small mini worlds where people in power do their best to shut up and shut out everyone who speaks truth to power. But the world is vast. There are areas where people do see each other for the value that each and every one brings to the table. There are people who strive for a just and equal world. There are people who care.

Hers is an American survival story. It is a triumph of sorts. They could not kill her off that easily.

Botched

Evaluation Procedure – Fail

Let's evaluate each human performance.

Available Categories:

1) Poor
2) Good
3) Excellent

1) Poor performers are let go with a minimum 4-week severance pay to prevent them from speaking up.

2) Good – Everyone is good unless they are poor. Good can either do it all and show gratitude. Or good can do the bare minimum as long as he/she plays or they play his/her/their cards right.

3) Excellent – Only those at the top of the food chain can do excellent work. It's as simple as that.

The point of an evaluation process is to instill fear and insecurity. It is also clear that boundaries are set. There is no point of questioning corporate boundaries such as these.

Communication Style – Fail

She/He/They do not understand. Do you know what would happen if everyone asked to be treated fairly and equally. She/He/They do not understand that every employee must be treated with respect and dignity despite their pay scale or title.

Our world is what it is because for a very long time, from the beginning of time, people who have seen themselves as being too powerful, have believed that they hold other people's fates in their hands. That kind of power has terrible direct effects and long-term side effects. That kind of unchecked power is nothing to be proud of.

Power through fear is not real power. It is cowardice. Leadership is not about instilling fear. Success is not about shutting others out. Those who speak up may have a reason.

Negotiation Process – Fail

Let's take a basic negotiation scenario. There are two parties. One strong and one not as strong. The strong party represents a corporation. The other party is an employee representing herself/himself/themselves. The playing ground is not even but nothing is even. Life goes on even in an imbalanced and uneven reality.

The ask: full credit and fair compensation based on merit.

The response is delayed.
It is ignored.
It is dismissed.
It is denied.
Denial without any sound reason is questionable, isn't it?

Final Verdict Announcement – Fail

When there is a serious request based on facts, should it be dismissed just like that? It can. It happens all the time.

The final verdict is in:

No, we see no reason for change.

We inherited your position. You were inherited. Reach out to that other party over there. Maybe you had a deal with them. We do not have anything to do with you. We are not doing anything wrong. We see no reason why we should acknowledge your contribution in full and without reservation. There is no budget for fair compensation.

Separation Phase – Fail

It was their fault. No, it's not our fault, it's the other party's fault.

Entity no. 1 – The tight knit community. They know exactly how much they have benefited from your contribution. If they do not know, they will soon find out.

Entity no. 2 – The administrators. They claim no responsibility. They deliver the news: Request for change of status is denied.

Entity no. 3 – The Corporate. They make decisions with no connections. They confirm the final date of employment. They are credited with the decision-making power. They said no.

What party did you belong to: entity no. 1, 2 or 3? You don't know? How could you not know? You don't know, you lose.

Response Management – Fail

Any request must be addressed in a timely manner. Consider all implications including short term and long-term results. When a request is denied and the response is short of facts, then that's a failure.

Nobody has to believe in putting people before profit, you say. But maybe profit before people is costlier than anyone likes to admit.

Who is responsible for a botched response to a serious request for equal pay and equal treatment based on facts?

Is the corporate world more interested in preserving inequality and unfairness in the name of profit?

Do you believe initiatives that seemingly focus on equality, diversity and inclusion?

If you are told that your expectations for equal and fair treatment are in discord with corporate reality, then get out. That type of corporate experience will do you no good.

People treating other people with the most basic levels of consideration and respect cannot be that complicated of a process. No spreadsheets are required. No elaborate evaluation mechanisms are necessary. No need for PhDs or law degrees.

The botched rollout of a short-sighted, money saving plan may be a side effect of a system failure. However, no matter how intricate the system in place, there is always a human at the end of it all.

Humans keep failing humans in the name of profit.

The Only One

She asked her colleague if he was going to the private party after the event. He said that he was going to avoid that one for sure. He was going to avoid the man of the hour, the famous face whose name was well known in various elite circles. The accumulated power protected the man from being held responsible for his alleged criminal behavior. Her colleague was stunned that she did not know. Was she the only one with no knowledge of such stuff? Was she hiding in a cave all this time? No, she just worked. She never had any interest in gossip of any kind. But this was not gossip. This was worse, much worse, wasn't it? It certainly was. How could she be the only one not knowing how the world works and how the powerful stay in power?

Ruined

If you leave this job and this salary, you will be ruined. You have done the same thing for almost two decades. You have no real-world experience. You are part of a niche area. You have no connections. You have financial responsibilities. You have kids. You have no fancy degrees. A master degree from a distinguished but not an ivy league school in NYC does not hold much water apparently, does it? Are you done paying off your school loans? Just remember that you are doing this to yourself. You will be ruined.

Ah, you're not leaving this job. What do you think you're doing: insisting on a title and a salary to match your endless work responsibilities and performance level? They're telling you to keep playing their game as you always have. If you get out of here, don't expect anyone to stand by you.

Keyword to remember: ruined.

Capitalism 101

She is told that this is capitalism 101. How did she not know about the vicious ways of the capitalist world?

Was this capitalism, she asked? Was it? It seemed very much like communism. Everyone was equal in communism. Fake equal.

The little guy and gal worked for the common good in communism. The folks on the podium were so proud of the working people. They did not have to pay fair wages. They concentrated on building a propaganda machinery. There was a special kind of camaraderie and happiness that was deemed priceless in communism. It was all a lie. It fell apart. It crumbled.

How did she fall for this same type of absurdity? She – of all people – should have known better.

F*ck You

What kind of retribution are you looking for? That is a question that will stick with her for the rest of her life. A religious man asked her that question. Over the phone. No paper trail.

Fuck You! The exact words in the lips of a genius man who was awarded a generous NEA grant. He said FU to her over the phone. He followed up with a long email justifying his choice of words. No apologies. The NEA genius worked for a famous house of God in a famous town. The priest was put in charge to clean up after the NEA genius. He was not too pleased about it. But he had to protect the house of God and the NEA genius.

Her tight knit group offered no support. "What do you expect?" she was asked. *People are stressed. People lash out. The art world does not have sufficient funds. Some people fail with words. It's just words. Nobody got hurt. You live in the city. You hear FU all over the place, don't you? C'mon! Man up!*

TriBeCa Film Festival

Arvo Paert's *Passio* at Trinity Wall Street Church. Isabella Rossellini smiled at her. She recited the text. She did it better than anyone else.

Man hurts man. Man experiments with pain. Man takes pleasure in pain inflicting procedures. Women are part of freak shows. They are powerless. How much pain is bearable? How much suffering?

Art soothes the soul. The art world does not have to do any of that. The art industry might kill a few dreams. It might hurt a few souls. She felt hurt. Definitely broken. At least for the time being.

Finding Jesus

Seating outside on a cold winter day. It's about 3:30. Having a black coffee for lunch. A teenage girl with black hair sits next to you. She says, "hi". You say, "hi" back. It's her first trip to New York City. She is here with her church group. Finding Jesus is the best thing that happened to her, she confessed.

Her presence, as unexpected as it is, seems like a good sign. "Jesus loves all. Lost and Found". The girl stares at you looking lost and confused. You take another sip from your coffee, get up and wave goodbye. A strange encounter!

It's a complicated and weird world. You feel betrayed. You walked a long stretch of your life side by side with a small group of people. Now you go your separate ways. Finding what you are looking for is not supposed to be easy. Finding meaning. Finding purpose. Feeling lost is part of the deal. It's what being human is all about.

Opportunities

Open to join new groups if all participants are truly treated equally and fairly.

Open to learn new programs and skills if full credit and fair compensation is given to every deserving team member.

Open to be fully invested in any team if respect and dignity are part of daily interactions and not only on company websites.

Open to development opportunities if merit-based performance is not muted in order to spotlight only the top brass shining brightly.

Open to strategizing, ideating, initiating and leading if there is full commitment to equality, diversity and inclusion.

E-Shame

She quit. Did she? Was she fired? Did they let her go only to make it look like she resigned? What a mess!

How many people were included in the final note that she sent out? Only five? There you go. She sent separate emails to others. Many colleagues sent her heartfelt notes. Everyone was confused. It was so sudden. It looked muddy. Her replies did not shed light on what happened exactly. She was not going to receive a reference letter from either of the companies in her signature. That ugly?

The Power of Narrative

During zoom and teams calls on Black Out Day and monthly meetings many expressed their frustrations with the levels of inequality and lack of diversity in the publishing industry. Real people were hurt by consistent and persistent closed-minded choices. Nobody knew why it had taken so long to consider change. Change was overdue.

Most of those who spoke up in defense of change had chosen to play the role of bystanders by default until those meetings. Finally, they realized that it was beneficial to express their feelings. They were hurt, too. It was hard seeing their friends and colleagues get ignored for so long. The born-again righteous intellectuals wanted to be part of the solution. Some of the loudest voices were those who were previously easily appalled by simple questions asked by *the others* who sounded and looked different. What uncontained excitement! Simply talking about inclusion initiatives was pure excitement.

Did you believe any of it? Not quite. You knew what it felt to be seen and called appalling and intimidating by these enlightened intellectuals. Nobody offered you an apology for the unsolicited and inexcusable personal attacks. You received a couple of excuses by third parties. "It's not that you are intimidating, it's that some of us are sensitive. Your confidence level and your performance level are intimidating to some, appalling even..."

Dishonesty is easy to detect. It is difficult to understand. It is overwhelming.

Today's loud crowd is speaking on behalf of the others who have little chance of getting a fair share of recognition for their contributions. Today's loud crowd is yesterday's disinterested crowd. The loud crowd was easily appalled and intimidated yesterday. Today they speak up on behalf of those who have been unfairly denied a voice for too long.

Owning narratives is power. Can you imagine the level of sacrifice and heroism belonging to those who claim ownership of the others' narratives?

The industry has been suffering for a while. This was a good time to embrace change. Controlled change. To a certain degree. Embrace a member of the BIPOC, LGBTQ+ and immigrant community. Embrace women from different spectrums. Take a picture with them. Tell their stories. Save the world! Ah, you saviors of the intellectual community! Ah, how deep goes your suffering for *the others*!

Prayer

They say a prayer for her/his sinful soul. They are saddened. They are utterly disappointed.

Why do small and insignificant subjects like me fail so miserably? This is basic stuff. It is easy to understand. Insignificant people cannot ask for full credit or fair compensation. Silly subjects like me and contributions like mine are part of some kind of inheritance. We are inherited. We get what we are given. We should move along with our heads held low.

What about showing some gratitude to a few powerful men? Those who dictate the fates of irrelevant minions are the ones who rule, pray, and decide.

It's game over for anyone who doubts the power of prayer from the lips of powerful demigods. Demigods have no time to waste with prayers for ungrateful dissenters.

Are you a deserving soul?
Then keep serving with gratitude.

The Great Resignation

People are resigning left and right. Why? Because there is:

Lack of leadership
Lack of understanding
Lack of effective communication
Lack of fair distribution of responsibilities
Lack of equal compensation
Lack of appreciation
Lack of desire to see things as they are
Lack of true and tested values
Lack of basic care for fellow humans

There are plenty of top tier executives who give monologues highlighting their greatness. Their cushy behinds are well protected and well cared for and that's all that matters.

There are many HR gurus and Chiefs of People who do not see people. They serve companies. They are corporate. The HR Department does not see humans. Profit is the only thing that corporate considers.

Have you heard Steve Harvey's take on DMV? Human Resource Departments might as well be the DMV of the corporate world. The corporate world is another worldly world that does not care about humans.

The corporate world gets busy mismanaging resources and profits. Then they compose and distribute plenty of fluffy initiatives about fairness, equality, diversity and inclusion. Those initiatives are part of the game. The corporate system is too rigid to care about change.

Low Expectations

What the fuck did you expect? The Chief of People to care about you? Did you think even for a minute that the SVP and the VP would take you seriously? Don't you fucking know that equal pay is not a real thing? It might be in Colorado. Not in New York. Equality does not work in New York. It stresses the system. You worked hard. What the fuck! You always worked hard. What has changed now? Why change now? Do you even know how many people in the world work hard? Many people work much harder than you, do you know that? Your station in life is decided by others. Own it bitch! Do you know how many more women, who are more skilled and more educated than you, never speak up. They accept their fate and go about their lives.

You are a low level nobody. You should demonstrate only low expectations. That's your only way to avoid being cancelled. Take note: low expectations from now on.

Confidential

There is nothing you can do

If we abuse your trust
If we exploit your dedication
If we take advantage of your honesty
If we nickel and dime you
If we shortchange you
If we offer you the option to have no health insurance
If we give you the opportunity to skip your vacation time
If we tell you to never share salary information with colleagues because it is illegal
If we do not acknowledge in writing the list of tasks that you do for the company
If we avoid to credit your work and achievements fully and properly
If we make statements to intimidate you
If we play around until we shut you out
If we talk about equality, diversity and inclusion but do not actually mean change
If we see ourselves as helpless bystanders when we know that we can take steps to make a difference
If we overlook your achievements, cap your earnings and increase your list of responsibilities constantly

Be aware that all of the above are confidential matters between the company and its subjects. A subject like you is of no consequence. It never was. It never will be.

Exotic Bird

How many cocktail parties did you attend as a special guest? "You are an exotic bird. Embrace that! Don't blend in!" Someone older and wiser advised you a while back. She noticed your level of discomfort. She wanted to help you fly higher. You wanted to believe her. But you never felt particularly exotic. You couldn't blend in. No matter what you wore, how little you spoke. You were/are a wallflower.

Cocktail parties with a busy smoked salmon station and cheap wine were a pain. Fake laughter and fake friends kissing each other were a real thing. Cocktail parties with special themes and special guests were not your thing. Too dry and cold of an atmosphere everywhere. Guest lists of countless phony people pretending to care about the world but certainly didn't and couldn't, really.

If you had paid attention and tried to connect with a few people here and there at a fancy cocktail party, you wouldn't have to apply for jobs now, would you? You would only have to phone a friend or ask for a favor. You won't have to complain about a boring cocktail party now, will you? You have no pending invitations to special cocktail parties. Don't expect any, anytime soon, our darling exotic bird.

Pronouns

He told her that they inherited her.

How could she be inherited? Inheritance usually implied nonliving things.

She did not feel like a "She" from Monday to Friday. She felt like a "She" some days. She felt like a "He" or even an "It" most days. She was like an AI entity who said 'thank you' every time she was given the honor to do everyone else's work. Nobody cared about how much was too much for her to manage. She felt like a "they" some days. She'd hear, "What is it to them?" even though it was only 'her'; never "them."

She knew that they did not care about her. She knew that she was unnoticeable despite her muted feelings and added pronouns. As long as she did all the work, the rest was noise.

She did not believe him. That was another he.

There were two teams. Or maybe three. It was never clearly defined. She was aware of 3 team members who had added "She" as their pronoun of choice on their signatures. She spoke to two of them twice. She saw one of them at senior management meetings. She never saw the third "she" member. The three "he" members were from different teams. All three denied having anything to do with the final decision. All three said that she was never part of their teams. She did not believe either one of them. They all lied.

Pronouns do not really make a difference if humans decide not to see humanity in one another.

Fleeing

She thought she had made an impression. Yes, she had. That of an idiot. Was she part of a special class? No. The world was full of idiots like her, she was told. She had nothing to complain about. Gratitude was the only thing she should have shared. All she had to do now was flee. Fleeing was her only option to save herself. She was wounded. Time heals all wounds, they say.

Was she better off? She was fleeing the ugliness of a world where lies are common and genuine feelings are rare and far in between.

Promotions

You've been promoted over the years. Don't deny it!

Initially a pussy.
Nobody feared you. You looked like a scared little pussy.

Later a bitch.
Doing plenty and covering all bases. Setting standards. What a bitch!

Then a whore.
Insisting on respect and dignity. What a whore!

Finally, a cunt.
Succumb to the will of the highest powers, that's all you had to do. You dared to make a move. Such a c-level move!

Smell Test

If it smells like shit. It looks like shit. It feels like shit. It's got to be shit. It doesn't matter if you didn't do it but only knew of it. It doesn't matter that you were not involved with it directly but were complicit. Who cares if the other team blames you and you blame the other team. The shit is there for you all to deal with. Enjoy!

Google Sheets

Did you feel drained, mentally, emotionally and physically consumed after two weeks of isolation as a result of Covid-19?
Did you feel exhausted and overwhelmed? Did anyone care?
Did you get back to work after the tenth day? Twelfth day?
Did you feel like you wanted to die at the sight of over a thousand emails and tens of voicemails?
Did you feel ashamed for letting things fall apart by being out for 2 weeks?
Did you feel abandoned during and after those two weeks?
Did it help getting Google Sheets prioritizing the hundreds of priority requests?
Did you feel like none of it was worth it? Did you cry?
Did you feel like part of you died from lack of empathy and lack of camaraderie?
Did you feel like reminding your team that showing some of their team spirit would be greatly appreciated during unusual times like these?
Did you feel like an idiot-in-chief? Did you realize that it was time to give up that special honor?
Did you feel anything about anyone who insisted on saving the status quo?

It was not their fault. It never is. You get the hell out. Let them disown you. Let them eat their google sheets!

IDGAF – the Corporate Edition

I am being squeezed to death here by the long list of responsibilities that I must cover without getting full credit in addition to fair and equal pay for my work.

Chief of People and HR: IDGAF

VPs & SVPs: IDGAF

Presidents (Past/Present) & Major Deal Makers: IDGAF

If IDGAF is the motto around here, then let's call it a day.

If you get excellent work reviews by clients who have been in the industry for longer than you have been alive as well as by newcomers who praise you for your relentless support and dedication, then they better not advertise their IDGAF positioning.

Old music. New Music. No Music. Just noise. IDGAF – Corporate Edition offered generously in the midst of the great resignation. *How visionary!*

Realizations

When you realize that the end of a long chapter of your life was long overdue.

When you realize that friendships dissolve instantly when minimum levels of honesty are unavailable by choice.

When you realize that when you give up prioritizing other people's priorities, a massive freak out is unavoidable.

When you realize that people who should have known better, know nothing at all and they flaunt their ignorance.

When you realize the oceans of difference between hearing someone say "I care about you" and seeing someone actually care about you.

When you realize that you "being special" was code for "fine to be exploited" label.

When you realize that people's food and drink choices are weaponized as misleading profile statements.

When you realize that your pain means nothing to those who are the root cause of your pain.

When you realize that backstabbing is a preferred pastime activity for many.

When you realize that you have made a difference and some won't write you off as yesterday's news.

Brooklyn Accent

Do I have a Brooklyn accent? I sure do. Brooklyn has many accents. Mine is one of them. If my accent gives you reason to doubt the power of my word, it's on you. The power of my actions speaks volumes. I am not a Brooklyn coward. I am one of Brooklyn's best. I like my Brooklyn accent. I will cherish my long list of colleagues and friends around the world.

If you tell me, take a seat and we'll never call you, then my Brooklyn spirit awakens. No, sir. I will not take a seat. I will let you play your own games with yourself. Have a good time with your sad crew. I'm taking my sweet Brooklyn soul out of this stagnate universe of yours.

Tanglewood

Giggles and laughter. Mosquitos are annoying but manageable. Drinking wine, listening to music, chasing stars. Meeting friends. Making new acquaintances. Getting away from the world while also trying to understand life through music. It is such a perfect setting.

There are many great summer music festivals around the country. Tanglewood is my favorite. Special memories. Fun times. Good sounds.

Music is wonderful especially when you are not aware or manage to forget the drama that goes on behind the scenes.

A Lil' Bit

Words
The thing is that I'm giving away a whole lot of myself. I am wasting away. I am not expandable to infinity and beyond. I am fully aware that I deserve more than a lil' bit of this and a lil' bit of that. I deserve my fair share.

Yeah but ...
A lil' bit of this and a lil' bit of that and there you go, you have two lil' bits of this and that. It is not much of this or that but it is not nothing. You could have nothing at all.

Majority of you people have nothing at all.

Keep in mind that you're replaceable. In fact, a few calls were made already.

212 Area Code

Her
You had a 212-area code and gave it up. How come? What's wrong with you? People pay loads of money to get a 212-area code.

Me
That's a way to look at it. Maybe the negotiators thought I'd die before giving up my 212-area code work number. I never even thought of it.

Her
You had an office in Manhattan.

Me
There was an office by MSG. I won't miss it. The other office is elsewhere. I never got to see it. I was told that it is a large space full of cubicles. I won't miss having a cubicle.

Her
An office in Manhattan, though. And a 212-area code.

Me
That's what employers think: give them a phone number, give them a cubicle, snacks, coffee and suffocate them with work. Work. More work.

If you have access to all that free stuff – cubicle, phone, snacks, coffee - you better feel privileged. But none of it is free though. It's your life that you are giving away in exchange. Your own damn life.

Her
Ingrates! Each and every one of you who complain about work. What else is there to do?

Me
Be treated with respect. Get credit for every single task that you do. Get compensated fairly. But they said, "no need for fair pay because we are already generously offering you a 212-area code, an office in Manhattan, snacks, and coffee."

Blood and Tears

There was no blood. There were tears. There were sweaty days. The AC never worked properly on the top floor. The heat was on and off at times. There was no heat in the women's bathroom. That was the old office. The new office was said to be a huge improvement. Key word: cubicles.

There was no time for boredom. Plenty of issues to address. Missing pages. Wrong data. Delayed shipments. Last-minute project changes. Too many invoices to be coded, approved and sent for payment. Enough charging and recharging to make anyone dizzy. It was a long-time spent strategizing, planning and managing every little detail affecting small and big productions in North America and other countries around the world.

It was not lonely. However, it was a lonesome endeavor at times. Nobody really chipped in to assist even when they got paid to do so. Everybody got an A for effort even if they didn't bother trying. You got noticed for doing it all and saying "please and thank you." Remember when you started off in 2005? You were one of two full time assistants. There were 2 directors in 2005. In 2022, you were one director with no assistants. You did everything that was done by 2 directors and 2 assistants in 2005. You did more. The roster was much bigger in 2022. Still, there was no budget to acknowledge all the work that you did. There was no budget for assistants. They were looking for a part-timer who would automatically get an A for effort even if s/he did not bother trying.

No joy left. You were a fun-loving human in 2005. No blood was spilled but your heart is broken now. You'll shed a few tears. If anything happens to you, you will not accept their thoughts and prayers. If they send any. As of now, you are disowned.

C'mon! Enough talking about your work from morning till night. It's over. It may take a while, but this, too, will pass.

Around Here

One of my overseas colleagues asked me if I started out with 5 or 6 weeks of vacation time. When I said, no way, no how, she seemed puzzled. Couldn't I negotiate my vacation time? No. During my 17 years of work, I never got to enjoy a 5-week vacation period.

I didn't even ask about vacation time during my initial interview. I was told that it was frowned upon to ask about vacation time.

Around here, things are done differently. Unless you work for a big player, you don't expect more than basic offerings.

I often heard complaints about unions. They said that unions make life harder for people who want to get stuff done.

Around here, there is no reason to worry about unions. You will be taken advantage of and written off as "the people who want to get stuff done" see fit.

In theory, everyone cheers for the working class. Isn't it awesome that this group of workers is trying to unionize? Isn't it cool that restaurants are sharing tips with the kitchen staff? Wasn't I told that I made more than a firefighter one time when I asked to be paid fairly for all the work that I did? Around here, I was not risking my life and I was given the chance to be part of a cultured scene. It was an elite scene. Wasn't that sufficient?

Survey

How do you rate your experience with this company?
How do I rate my experience with the company, you ask?

On a scale of 0 to 10.
What do you think? Take a wild guess.

Explain why.
No one within the company never even bothered to connect with me, let alone acknowledge the magnitude of my contribution. The company goes against its own values. What is at the basis of the company culture here? Fear! Submission! Silence!

Ha! How do I rate my experience with HR? LMT...
This HR Department can be easily substituted by an automated service. All HR did was send automated emails about mental days, holidays, and generic forms. There was no human interaction of any kind. What is human resource management?! If anything, this HR is responsible for depletion of available human resources.

Would you recommend this company to your friends?
What do you think? Friends help each other. Would I be a good friend if I sent someone here? This company looks after only a few people at the top. I'll tell my friends about my experience.

Take Care/Give Care

What does it mean to take care and to give care?
One of my old colleagues shared this line. It is a good reminder that serves anyone who pays attention.

What does it mean to take care and to give care? It means to do good, to be helpful, to be fair, to be considerate. That's how you take care of yourself and others. That is the only way you move forward and do your part by contributing to a better tomorrow.

You may go up the food chain quicker if you lie and cheat and cut in line. But achievements that are not based on merit, have weak or no foundations. Don't you agree? If no, why not?

How much do we gain if we take shortcuts and indulge in instant gratification without the slightest consideration of what lies ahead?

Our world is what it is because people continue to avoid taking care/giving care. Small acts make a difference.

If we forget our common humanity, then what are we left with? Change is good even if it is inconvenient to those who benefit from the status quo. Can you imagine a world where we really take care/give care just because...

Missing Part

What part will I miss the most?

I won't miss the July birthday wishes. I am an Aquarius.
I won't miss the fake humility through stories and anecdotes of people who bend the truth as a sport.
I won't miss fake friendship circles and insincere discussions about world peace.
I won't miss the silly care packages with fancy jelly beans and cheesy inspirational messages.
I won't miss the pretend top-secret details about unimportant stuff.
I won't miss doing everyone's work and cleaning everyone's messes.
I won't miss the automated feel-good emails from HR.

I will miss my good friends in all 50 states and beyond. My hands were shaking every time I replied to their farewell notes. I received the kindest messages from remarkable professionals who have been in the business for longer than I have been on planet earth. Many newcomers to the industry took the time to reach out and say thank you for my helpfulness and support. I will miss daily interactions with amazing people who do so much and who have taught me so much. I will miss my colleagues who always stood by my side when I needed them most.

Spiegel im Spiegel

A fine mirror broken into a thousand pieces. A delicate image dissolved by stubborn words. Heavy tears reflected in sharp angles. Red eyes. Swollen lips. Lifeless limbs. Unspoken sadness. The weight of disappointment set aside but not easily erased by time.

Proceed with Caution

The road ahead is full of unknown elements. If you are a woman, the list of unknowns is longer. If you have no fancy educational background or well-connected network to rely on, the obstacles awaiting you are considerable. But keep moving and listen to your heart. There are plenty of fake friends and phony characters to meet along the way. They will embrace you if embracing you means bonus points for them. They will make you believe that they care about you as long as you serve their bottom line. The moment you speak up, the moment you demand to be treated fairly and equally, you will find out who is a real friend and who is a temporary name in your contact list.

Do not feel guilty or ashamed asking to be credited in full for your contributions. Do not back down from asking for fair and equal compensation. Even people and institutions that embrace equality, diversity and inclusion in written form, may fail to live up to their promises in real time. Remind them of their promises. Be persistent!

If the SVPs and VPs of your corporate world tell you to your face that they see no reason for change, then consider your options. Don't be discouraged. Do not give up asking for equal pay, fair treatment and full acknowledgement of your work. You deserve better than a status quo that benefits your circle but keeps you stuck in place. If you choose to leave, you are not leaving as a quitter. You are leaving to continue your search for a place and a tribe that value you based on who you are and what you contribute.

Proceed with caution. The hero's journey is hard. The heroine's journey is harder.

Do not fall for intimidation tactics to keep you tied down. Do not allow anyone to mess up with your sense of self. If you work hard and if you do good, you will be fine. It sucks to cry. Cry away for a while. Get up. Move on. Take small steps or run. You know what pace fits you best. Live with integrity.

One day, after a karate class, my little one came home and shared what he had learned. How I loved hearing him say the golden rules to live by: Work hard! Be persistent! Show fortitude! And never ever give up!

Life comes to an end for everyone. Every moment counts. Be aware of what you leave behind. Seize the moment. Keep moving. Proceed with caution and with faith.

Made in the USA
Middletown, DE
20 April 2022